View
from the
Rollercoaster

Unsteady Essays & Bipolar Bylines

Tracy Ebbert Revalee

ISBN: 061545254X
ISBN-13: 9780615452548

Contact the author at
www.viewfromtherollercoaster.com

TABLE OF CONTENTS

Liar, Liar, Pants on Fire 1
2011, Liberty, Indiana

Dr. J. Vernon McGee..3
1976, Santa Monica, California

Manic Boogie 7
1982, Alexandria, Virginia

Pine Street 9
1987, Richmond, Virginia

The Ghost of Exes Past..13
1988, Richmond, Virginia

Due Monday..17
1989, Richmond, Virginia

Certifiably Not Crazy...21
1994, Chesapeake, Virginia

In the Mall and In the Manger 23
2005, Liberty, Indiana

As Good As It Got 27
2011, Liberty, Indiana

Dog Bites Reporter, Dog Lives 31
2002, Liberty, Indiana

The Pig Interview...33
2003, Liberty, Indiana

Breakdown 2004...37
2011, Liberty, Indiana

You're Saving My Life 47
1982, Alexandria, Virginia

Breast Cancer 49
2011, Liberty, Indiana

The Dune 53
1989, Duck, North Carolina

PREFACE

If you or someone you know lives with mental illness, this scenery may be familiar: mania, job-hopping, broken relationships and breakdowns. In this book, dated chapters will guide the reader through a journey of time, place and experience to the healing shelter of a dune by the sea. It's a non-linear trip, not unlike being bipolar.

You'll hear a lilting voice as you turn these pages. If it charms you, fine. Better yet if it persuades you that any life can be redeemed. I hope you enjoy putting your feet up and cruising these essays and columns at your leisure. They each stand alone but look for dates in the Table of Contents to orient yourself if the ride gets too frenetic.

Do sing the *Manic Boogie*. You can sing it to any tune—even *Twinkle, Twinkle, Little Star*. Does it move the story forward? Well, of course it does; it's one way to describe the euphoria of a manic episode. But that was for me to figure out. I just want you to enjoy the journey. Sing the silly song. Wander down a gentle Southern street. The meaning will come. Be patient.

While I hope there is much truth herein, this is not a true book. Memory fails, I'm aging and I continue to take prescription psychotropic drugs that affect the memory I do have. For nearly twenty years I numbed the pain of mental illness with … well, lots of things, none of which helped my memory.

But I do not let facts get in the way of a good story, so give me some leeway and I'll give you a tale.

LIAR, LIAR, PANTS ON FIRE

Liberty, Indiana—I once interviewed a man who had been struck by lightning. Actually, I interviewed his wife, because the man was hiding in the bathtub, both from me and from lightning. An early morning sprinkle of rain had so terrified him that he retreated into his fiberglass sanctuary, which he did whenever any weather event could result in a white flash from the sky.

Noting that the man lied to his boss in order to get time off to go to an amusement park with his kids, the editor made "Liar, Liar, Pants on Fire" our working title for the piece. It was published under a much less incendiary title.

After several hours of fun on the rides, an afternoon thunderstorm had brewed quickly. When it broke, the victim left his wife with the children as he sprinted to the car. Lightning struck within twenty feet of where he stood on the lot.

Violently, this young man's paradigm shifted. His entire approach to life was radically changed. He didn't sleep, he didn't eat and he didn't take telephone calls. His job, ironically, was as a telephone lineman. He had never been struck by lightning on the job, but he certainly did not consider returning to that line of work.

When I spoke with his wife, she said she was, of course, grateful that he survived but grieved his former happy-go-lucky spirit. She was thankful for his life but lived as a virtual single mother with a husband who was more fearful of getting caught in rain than their toddler was afraid of strangers.

Not only had his paradigm shifted but so had that of his wife, child and friends.

The first of my two life-changing paradigm shifts also happened in a parking lot. The second was in a psychiatric ward.

DR. J. VERNON MCGEE

Santa Monica, California—There were two unusual things that stay in my memory from the day I heard Dr. J. Vernon McGee on the radio. One was the car. Whose car was that, anyway? I know I never owned a car in the five years I lived in Los Angeles. I arrived in a plane and left on a whim and I never owned a car in between. So it must have been a borrowed car. Or maybe it belonged to the sailor I married in Los Angeles before I hurried home to Virginia.

Then there was the cheese sandwich. It was rare for me to think far enough ahead to make my lunch but I remember the taste of the cheese when my saliva simply dried up at the sound of the words that changed my life.

It *wasn't* unusual that I was listening to talk radio. All morning long the ringing phone, the whirr and ping of Selectric II typewriters and the overbearing snort of the mouth-breathing office manager had frayed my nerves. So, much as I love music, a speaking voice could be more relaxing during a short lunch in the parking lot.

But not this voice!

His accent was a broad Texas twang, his delivery was fast but never hurried and he projected complete certitude that the Bible was true in every sense. I'm sure I wasn't the first or last person to whom Dr. McGee's sermons were life-changing. But somewhere between his trademark phrase, "May I say?" and the end of that day's *Thru the Bible* radio program, I began to consider a radical idea.

What if Jesus really is the way, the truth and the life and there is no other way to the Father but by him? (John 14:6)

What if the world really isn't an endless cycle of history but a story with a beginning, a middle and an end? What if Jesus is coming back in a solid, concrete and literal sense? (Rev. 1:7)

I knew from my church upbringing that Jesus was historical, radical, political and, among the religious elite of his day, heretical. Dr. McGee's careful verse-by-verse explanation of the Bible, beginning for me in that day in the parking lot, flashed a white light across the brown Los Angeles sky: What if Truth with a capital T could be found in the Bible?

If so, would it save my life, or ruin it?

The implications of a literal hell dried my mouth. I was living a life steeped in darkness, in a dank and smoky place where my spirit had been drowning since I was a teenager. Still, I had the sense that God had my back, that I was a good enough person to enjoy the presence of light and joy through eternity. It was chilling to think that I could be wrong.

The implications of a literal heaven raised my eyes. What would it look like to feel simple happiness without fear that the next day would bring inexplicable, infinite pain.

Pain had always been the way. Nothing in my life should have caused the hellish depressions I experienced in my youth. Even as I began to use cigarettes, alcohol, drugs, food and bad boys to numb the pain, I was an excellent student and musician. Those activities were enough to keep me out of trouble but not enough to bring satisfaction or peace. The idea of a place of rest and peace, simple joy and honest laughter—heaven—gave me something to think about.

I had always talked to God but I had never understood how to listen. In fact, my one-way communication with the creator of the universe was often as trusting and worshipful as a child. When I had moods that could cast me from mud holes to rainbows in an evening, I felt I could talk to him like the toddler who is not understood by anyone but her mother. I knew, too, that I could be angry at God. I had been taught that He is big enough to be challenged.

After that day in the parking lot with Dr. McGee I began to read the Bible seriously. In time, I came to realize that it was nothing less than His primary means of speaking to me. Not that I've always listened, but the beginning of two-way communication began in a parking lot in a borrowed car, with a half-eaten cheese sandwich and God's voice coming over the speakers.

MANIC BOOGIE

Tracy Elizabeth Vowell Prentiss Ebbert is a bipolar singer/songwriter/secretary posing as a bubbly charming light-hearted bon vivant in various parts of Virginia, California, Ohio, New Jersey and Florida. She is desperately ill and should be considered a danger to herself.

Alexandria, Virginia
The other day I was baking a cake
I mowed the lawn and I watered and raked
I made you a present I was wrapping the bows
While I was on the phone I was changing my clothes
In a few spare moments I wrote this tune
I was on a roll and it wasn't even noon.
    I'm manic, I'm manic, Not hyper or over aggressive
    I'm a full-blown manic depressive.

Took two minutes flat to mop the floor
I made some curtains and painted the door
I flew to Toledo and I brought you back
I met you on the plane and I had an attack.
    I'm manic, I'm manic, Not hyper or over aggressive
    I'm a full-blown manic depressive

I ran twenty-seven miles on the treadmill machine
And I went on a thousand dollar shopping spree
I hope the bank doesn't cash that check
But I'm just a little numb and I don't give a heck.
    I'm manic, I'm manic, I'm not hyper or over aggressive
    I'm a full-blown manic depressive.

PINE STREET

Tracy Ebbert is not quite starving to death in a garret in Oregon Hill. She is an editor, singer/songwriter and a near-graduate of Mary Baldwin College's Adult Degree Program.

Richmond, Virginia—When you're passing through, so many places leave no marks on the psyche, merely serving as backdrops to the traveler's stage of life; they are remembered only as scenery.

And then there is Oregon Hill. This one hundred eighty year-old urban neighborhood welcomes the stranger. Residents old and young spend hours talking politics on the front porch, offering advice on pruning a rose bush, or sharing memories of how the neighborhood eked out its living during the Depression. Although some might want to think this is what small town America is like, my subsequent travels have convinced me that Oregon Hill is a singular and precious jewel.

According to residents, Oregon Hill is bordered on the north by Cary Street. Although the Richmond Metropolitan Access expressway severed the northern part a decade ago, you can't prove it by those whose homes share both sides of The Ditch. Belvidere Street to the east, Hollywood Cemetery to the west and the James River are the less debatable borders.

Though Oregon Hill has one of the lowest crime rates and some of the best examples of nineteenth century row houses in Richmond, recent news coverage has only focused on Oregon Hill's proximity to Virginia Commonwealth University. The University seems to see the Hill as a natural annex to its cobbled-together urban campus. The neighborhood is also a brisk twenty-minute walk from the business and professional district downtown. These geographic facts account for its value, but what of its character? Some of that character resides in the commercial establishments on the corners. Care to stroll?

The Pine Street Barber Shop doubled its floor space last year by moving from 324 to 334 South Pine Street. Five stylists stand before the new mirrors on a Saturday morning, trimming, shampooing, rolling, coloring and blow-drying hair.

The stereo floats soft jazz through the shop. Original art clings to two walls and a collection of old apothecary jars fills one of the glass cases on the third wall. The street-side wall's east-facing windows admit bright blocks of morning sunlight.

Above the syncopated broadcast beat and the chatter of waiting clients, the telephone rings every ten minutes or so. The answer is usually the same: "Not today.

I'm sorry, we're booked. May I arrange another time for you?"

Delia's Kitchen at the intersection of Pine and Spring Streets reflects none of the prosperity of the barber shop, but it's a fine place to get a serious breakfast. Three coffee pots are emptied and refilled by Delia's quick hands, and at least ten customers are seated in front of Delia's Special: Two eggs, bacon or sausage, hash browns, biscuits or toast—all hot, all homemade, all for $4.25.

Delia's pine and plaster walls bear blown-up photographs of the neighborhood children dressed up in spanking new discount-store finery. They shine with parental pride from every wall. Even though the door faces west, the setting sun can't rival the children's faces for brightening the windowless room.

The closest place to Delia's to buy a morning paper is Majors Market. At Majors, there is no attempt at decoration. The air is still, dark and timeless, even on the brightest September morning.

A very young woman carrying a toddler on her hip purchases milk. A still-younger woman buys Marlboros in the hard pack. Six teenagers buy two soft drinks between them. The cashier purses her thin lips and looks hard at the boys before she returns their change.

The market's customers are the people of Oregon Hill as many native Richmonders stereotype them. But they are no more or less typical than the customers at the barber shop who come from all over the city for

Pine Street's special flair, nor than the young college-educated professionals who are buying and renovating the row houses there.

Although you may have heard that it is poor and dis-integrating, Oregon Hill is rich in diversity and made strong by the threads of tradition, family and churches woven throughout the community.

Oregon Hill is evolving and may surprise the larger community with its vigor and the weapons it brings to its fight for survival.

THE GHOSTS OF EXE'S PAST

Tracy Ebbert writes her column, Second Wind, specifically for non-traditional students of Virginia Commonwealth University. She attended VCU during an unspecified previous decade of her life and returned in 1987.

Richmond, Virginia—In the spring you get showers, in the summer it's mosquitoes and this time of year you get those pesky ghosts.

Of course since you're an adult and you've got good sense, you're not afraid of ghosts. Not the kind that come out of the grave on All Saints' Eve, anyway. But when the maples turn golden and the days grow brief, some ghosts seem to have the power to make you feel, if not haunted, at least gloomy.

The Ghost of Outfits Past lurks in the closet. His voice rustles when you pull the tissue paper out of a carefully stored sweater, only to find an intrepid moth got there first. Try on the matching pants before you pay to re-weave the sweater; you may well find the Ghost of Too Many Cookies. That's his shadow obscuring your toes.

Ghosts take many forms, but goblins are invariably mischievous and ugly. There's no hard evidence on this but I think there is an uncanny correlation between Halloween and the emergence of politicians from their usual haunts and into our television screens as the leaves turn. It has been said that Satan is a liar. It seems his minions in the realm of elected politics emulate his style. That's not just my opinion; that's what they say about each other. Okay, maybe they aren't all Satanic creatures, maybe they're just creepy.

Non-traditional students (that's "older" for all you straight-talkers out there) have unique ghosts. Some of us have the voice of an ex-husband or wife whispering out of the past.

"You're taking statistics? You couldn't even balance the checkbook!" Much as you might want to show off your academic achievements to your ex, might I be so bold as to suggest you leave that old carcass right there in whatever personal Memorial Garden you have buried it? Some things are just too painful to exhume.

Maybe thoughts turn to death and gloom because the greenery of summer is dying all around. A plunging thermometer shouldn't necessarily signal similar plunging moods. Think of the season as a sloughing of the old, dry skin and an opportunity to grow. Specters of the past can only slow you down.

A second, third or fifth chance at higher education is a cool, fresh breeze through your life. Wrap your memories around you like the cedar scented quilts pulled from summer storage. Make them your servants rather than the masters they would be, and, as my aerobics instructor would say, when things start to get you down, exorcise.

DUE MONDAY

Richmond, Virginia—Emerging into the late summer sunshine on Friday afternoon, who has any more ambition than to relax, rejuvenate and recharge for two days? The beach calls, the river beckons, the mountains offer cool respite from the overheated city.

The freshman class has survived the first week of class. We pretty much know where classes are held and what the professors look like. Not physically (who cares?) but as in, "Looks easy" or "Looks tough" or "Looks like I might consider changing my major." By Wednesday, we realized a mildly threatening look to some of the faculty, a hint of the reptilian under the shiny balding head, but surely they have our best interests in mind, yes? Hah!

By Friday, the true state of affairs is obvious. The professors are going to kill us.

It's due Monday. This Monday. Everything. Everything is due Monday.

Every Ph.D has spoken and assigned something huge. It's due Monday. This Monday. Everything. Everything is due Monday.

Our roommates are still virtual strangers. We could hang out but it's due Monday. What about Saturdays and Sunday? Don't we get a break?

Well, no. The classes are crowded and the competition is strong. You will not have twenty-four hours of your own, no less a whole weekend, until spring break. And even then you may have a sadistic professor who wants results at the end of that so-called vacation.

How can we carve out time for ourselves, our souls, our friends, our Oreos?

The problem is, you came this far with a certain set of habits and assumptions that helped you survive, a certain set of givens that defined your lifestyle. But now that you've taken on the burden of additional formal education, let's face it: Those habits have become little demons.

It might have been important to you as you were in the earlier years of your life that your house was dazzling, shining with Mr. Clean-like rays of blue white cleanliness. That was part of your identity then but could it be that you might have traded in that priority for a student ID? So let's start with house pride.

1. First, do no harm. Has a dust bunny ever actually bitten your toes? Of course not; leave the poor thing be.

2. What happens when you vacuum? You just have to vacuum again! Does this not sound like a vicious cycle of dust paranoia and dust retaliation? Should you lower yourself to battle with infinitesimal gray matter? Hardly.

3. At what point does your bathroom mirror truly offend? Sure, other surfaces do probably need

bacterial protection, but what're a few toothpaste splats on the mirror?

To each his own in regard to personal care, but some of the principles above can be used in delineating pure hygiene from pure vanity. Pay attention to principle No. 2 as it regards the application of moisturizing creams. At the risk of sounding glib, gravity is inevitable and so are wrinkles. Get ahead of the game. Adopt that slightly disheveled look as your own. Embrace it, own it and be proud.

If others object, hear them out with the greatest forbearance, nodding sagely when they complain that you're letting yourself go. While it is very important to look concerned it is even more important not to promise any improvement.

Just remember, those professors are looking for something on Monday and they probably don't care how you look when you turn it in.

CERTIFIABLY NOT CRAZY

Tracy Ebbert is divorced. Again.

Chesapeake, Virginia—She's at home anywhere—and out of place everywhere.

She's a straight skirt, silk blouse and navy blue pumps sort of girl and wouldn't pierce or tattoo any part of her body on a bet.

She's also capable of spending the day un-showered, in her pajamas and appearing that way at the grocery store, although she'll usually put on her "Sanctified (holy) Sweater" over the pajamas for the trip.

She has recovered from: alcohol, cocaine, marijuana and cigarettes, marrying alcoholics, addicts, abusers and worse.

She is still in thrall to the music of female singers and songwriters and to all children related to her by blood or marriage. She's a puppet on a string whether it be pulled by Bonnie Raitt or her own grandchild.

Despite the assertions of three husbands, several roommates and her entire family of origin, she is certifiably not crazy.

She is manic depressive, sure, but "...able to manage her own illness responsibly," according to a letter produced by a psychiatrist during the child custody dispute with her daughter's father.

She won.

In so many ways, by the sweet grace of God, she won.

IN THE MALL AND IN THE MANGER

Liberty, Indiana—"Have you done your Christmas shopping yet?"

It isn't yet November as I write and this seems to be a popular, if not incessant, question.

The appropriate answer is: (apologetically) "I haven't even started yet!" Anything short of this good-humored regret brands you irresponsible but at least humble.

But I don't do humble well, especially in regard to shopping. Shopping is distasteful and I don't mind revealing this attitude to dear friends. However, when this sensitive topic is raised by a stranger; I tend to reply with a tight-lipped "No."

I should say here that if I have a goal in life, that goal is to be a grumpy old woman. I like them and I aspire to be one. So far I'm just selfish and opinionated, but give me time.

So, with this goal in mind, how I ache to answer the Christmas shopping question self-righteously, just so I can see the inquisitor squirm. It's the curmudgeonly thing to do.

"No," I could say, "we won't be celebrating at my house until all the soldiers are back."

Or, how about this? "I won't be shopping this year, since I've already spent my disposable cash for relief to _____ (earthquake, tsunami, mud slide) victims." The ecologically correct answer will work, too, especially if pronounced with the gentle pity reserved for those who just can't seem to get the big picture about protecting the rain forests.

"I see no reason to shop with plastic for plastic that will end up in landfills, a third of which will be closed within two years due to excessive use of plastic."

While the shopping question brings out the humbug approach, I can't regard the holiday itself with any degree of cynicism because the message of Christmas is so powerful to me. Some claim the celebration was co-opted by my (Christian) tradition from an earlier (pagan) tradition. The logic seems to be that the popularity of those celebrations tempted the early church, so Christians simply hi-jacked the joyous rites, taking holly, berries, mistletoe and all.

While worse crimes have been committed in the name of public relations and increasing the membership roles, I think God's new deal would have engendered its own celebrations even if the pagans hadn't been in the mix.

The birth of Jesus signaled a change in the season of eternity. Before this birth, there was winter; man's best shot at justice was to demand an eye for an eye. His birth heralded the transcendence of divine justice, the

Judge asking only that we believe what this child would proclaim. (John 3:16)

There's hope in that message. There's hope for a season of personal and corporate renewal. There's hope for a world of understanding and peace.

So what's my Christmas shopping got to do with this? My question exactly. If Christmas is about spiritual history and the rebirth of innocence, what meaning resides in a shopping mall?

The meaning will be in the small tokens I can buy to express my gratitude for that Child and for your friendship. The meaning will be in the occasional peaceful face, probably the face of a child, whose expression is unblemished by the seasonal chaos.

If approached in the right spirit, the meaning in the mall can be transformative. Even for a curmudgeon-in-training, the mall can be a place of celebration. Though I haven't been there yet.

AS GOOD AS IT GOT

Tracy Ebbert Revalee is writing a book. It does not have a deadline. Her log home in Indiana houses books, photographs and musical instruments gathered during a lifetime of learning, traveling, singing and writing. She is the proud parent of one extraordinary child, step-mother to three amazing children and grandmother to six perfect grandchildren.

Liberty, Indiana—My first seven career starts were in food service, bartending, catalog sales, secretarial science, temporary clerical work, personnel recruitment and (who could forget) insurance underwriting. The insurance underwriting was more interesting than it sounds and it paid my rent in a pink stucco house I shared with a Mozart enthusiast and a David Bowie fan in Los Angeles. But I'm always restless and always curious, so I answered a classified ad in an insurance trade magazine published in Santa Monica.

"Writers wanted. Will pay for a way with words."

Although my employer at the insurance company discouraged my resignation from a 9-to-5 job in order to write, this has never been a winning argument with me. (At fifty years of age, I realized my resume was a train wreck but while I was running the rails I just didn't care.)

The Merritt Publishing Company was in the process of making insurance textbooks more "reader friendly" by turning their prose into snappy one- or two-liners suitable as educational filmstrip captions. I was asked to keep the prose at a fourth-grade reading level since that was considered the average reading level of working adults United States.

I could rewrite a couple of chapters a week and pay the rent. I didn't need big pay but I found a passion for fooling around with words. I was independent and no one's employee and I thought the whole arrangement idyllic.

It didn't take long, though, to write myself out of a job. I created more scripts than the company had budget to produce. Because I didn't have a degree, the editor was not able to hire me as a regular writer when the freelance work ran out.

By the time I did go to college, I had tried my hand at legal secretarial and paralegal work and fooled around with words and a guitar. Singing and songwriting fed the soul, paralegal work paid the bills.

I managed to get a bachelor's in Communications from a small liberal arts college, and at the same time wrote a weekly column for another university's newspaper. I was later offered an editorial position with the paper for a princely sum that would darn near buy a pair of jeans. Other editors asked me to write for their magazines and I did. I even got fan mail, which I kept with a growing clip file.

When I graduated I was pregnant with my first child. Fast-forward fifteen years—that seems to happen with the birth of a child—and that clip file came to light when I answered another ad, this time for a local weekly newspaper.

I wrote features, a column and the usual beat reporting, pitching in with photography and layout as required by a small newspaper.

The best thing that happened there was that my daughter saw journalism up close and personal, deciding eventually to make it her own career.

The worst thing was that my bipolar brain saw deadlines up close and personal and it decided to go over the edge in a big way.

DOG BITES REPORTER, DOG LIVES

Liberty, Indiana—Since the trauma forever removed the dog's real name from my mental address file, I'll call him Biter. Biter and I both lived this dramatic occurrence but I doubt it changed his life at all.

The day portended no danger, not even a headache. It was just a pleasant early autumn walk. When I passed Biter's house I noted there was a fence and I noticed Biter. He appeared to be having his own lovely doggy day. He was slobbering on his lady friends (I will not call them their biologically correct names), squatting on his owner's azaleas and eyeing his fence.

That means we had that one moment of intimacy, Biter and I, eyeing the fence between us. I, however, did not realize we had different intentions concerning each other and the fence.

See Biter run. Run, Biter, run. Squeezing his sleek body through the fence did not seem to be a new experience to him. He covered the ground between us in an instant.

Run, Reporter, run. But I couldn't. I was frightened into slow motion, my own screams ricocheting around my ears, my legs transformed to wood and my bladder dangerously close to the edge. And that was before all

Biter's colleagues showed up for the feast. He was definitely the lead singer but he had a mighty choir of menacing canines behind him.

At first, I did try a more assertive and less hysterical approach. I drew up to my full height and assumed the lowest, harshest, growliest voice I could find. I announced to Biter and his lady friends that I was a human and they were not. I was the master and they were the slavish canines long ago tamed by my forebears. I had a lovely, if enhanced, set of pearly whites and they had...TEETH. And scratchy little nails that felt like talons. And dog breath. They had sheer numbers. And, when it was all said and done, I had a dog bite.

Biter's owner finally came out of his farmhouse and herded the pack back behind its fence. He apologized. For all the drama on my part, I had a very large bruise and a very small bite and no real reason to sue.

According to the sheriff, dogs that bit were to be quarantined for ten days. According to my acute observational skills, justice was not served.

Biter never stayed in quarantine for ten minutes, no less ten days. He was out lapping dew from the fencepost and salivating when I drove by the next day. Not to be bitter, Biter, but you will not get a chance at this reporter again.

And to the editor who finally got a chance to write the headline, "Dog Bites Reporter, Dog Lives," you're welcome.

THE PIG INTERVIEW

Liberty, Indiana—Farmers and I live in very different worlds. We inhabit the same road, but I moved in from the suburbs. Never have I been so aware of this than the day I wrote the story that accompanied the picture of the pig kiss.

The principal of College Corner Union School had promised to kiss a pig if her students met certain reading goals during that grading period. I showed up at the auditorium in time to take a picture of the pig-kissing and then went to interview the pig. (The principal was busy.)

The pig was small and young and rather more stubbily than I thought it would be. It didn't seem any the worse for wear after its close encounter with the principal.

A middle-school student held the blanket-wrapped pig and I asked her what the pig was named. The little girl gave me a look of shock, disbelief and pity.

"We don't name the pigs," she said politely. She refrained from laughing. I was and am grateful for her self-control. She was kind to ignore the shame that I felt at that moment.

Naming the pig, indeed. I have a 4-year old nephew who would have known better than to ask the pig's name. In fact, he's probably up on quite a few things I don't know.

Fitting into a new culture can be uncomfortable but the only way to bridge the gap is by sticking around and paying attention, I guess. I'd ask more questions, but I sometimes think my farming neighbors would have more to say were they not completely dumbstruck by the unfathomable depths of my ignorance.

Moreover, it has been said you can't ask a fish what the water is like. I am not inclined to ask a fish anything but I believe the point is that the fish is so entirely one with the water that he would be unable to attain the necessary distance and objectivity to describe the aquatic atmosphere.

So it is with those who have lived life closer to the earth than to the edge.

How can I face my neighbor as she toils down her rows of tomatoes, while I pop out my front door to pick one tomato for a salad from my one tomato plant? She will can her tomatoes. I do not can, I cannot can, I can not one single fruit or vegetable.

Furthermore, the difference between hay and straw continues to escape me.

On one hand, I have learned that when they talk about beans around here, they generally refer to soybeans, not green beans. I spent my first several months of residence in Union County in a mild state of confusion about that issue.

And I do have a positive attitude. I knew when I moved to the country I would not necessarily be able to get out of my rural drive after a bad snow, so I don't complain.

In fact, I counted it great luck when the road on which we built our house was paved a few months after we moved in. It's one of the reasons I plan to stay around long enough to figure out the difference between straw and hay.

BREAKDOWN 2004

Liberty, Indiana—One hundred thirty-five pounds of well-toned muscle packed on a 5-foot 7-inch frame, not bad for forty-seven years old, I thought. My clothes weren't downright baggy but had a nice loose fit. I liked what the mirror said.

The mirror also said my eyes had dark gray rings under too-bright pupils, and protruding cheekbones. My skin tone and hair were both flat. I jittered. My thoughts felt like clouds of swirling seeds skittering across my brain. It was fall. The damp leaves and violent colors of the trees, cooling temperatures and amber sunsets teased my senses. I felt like a thoroughbred at the gate, nose to the wind, head in the race.

The important thing was this: I could fly. I didn't have hallucinations or delusions that I could physically rise into the air but I was convinced I could do with very little sleep, food or the bother of human interaction.

I could fly.

My 1998 Mustang really could fly, or at least as fast as country roads would allow. In retrospect, it's a good thing it only has a V-6 engine, or I would have driven faster. As it was, I burned rubber when I launched out of the garage every morning.

Since my husband wouldn't stay up with me to talk all night, I took my computer into the family room and wrote all night. He finally insisted I move my desk into our bedroom so we would at least be in the same room.

I fooled him. I talked to myself v-e-r-r-r-r-y quietly all night. I hammered at the keyboard, I got up and exercised (hence the well-toned muscle.) I started a million news articles but rarely was able to finish one. I read everything in our library and then started in on my daughter's books. I believed I really didn't need to sleep. In the middle of the night I felt the same buzzing grind of wakefulness and sharp ideas that I did mid-afternoon. Of all the half-lies I told my husband, the worst was that my newspaper job required all this late night work.

All this energy was producing less and less actual work product, since nothing actually was completed. My editor needed more copy and less drama. He fired me.

He did me an enormous favor.

I had been fired from a job. Usually, I quit before they caught on to my moods. Writing for a newspaper was what I was trained and educated for, what I could do all day long, what I was really good at. Now my illness had taken down a job I really cared about. I was devastated.

So I straightened up my act. I found a psychiatrist, entered an (outpatient) facility for the third time in my life, and made up my mind to make it work. I just didn't want to live like that anymore.

I'm not saying a simple decision to straighten up is sufficient to control or defeat mental illness. My experience is that the better I treat my body and the more honest I am with mental health professionals, the healthier I get. My testimony is that I could not have made the decision nor stuck by it day after day, year after year, without the Holy Spirit's guidance.

That experience of choosing to accept God's healing through medicine was the second paradigm shift.

If I were less stubborn, it could have happened twenty-five years earlier when I was going through an agonizing depression after my second divorce. I was suicidal again. When I admitted myself this first time to the psychiatric floor of a local hospital, I was fantasizing that I could run my car off the road into an abutment. I had the particular abutment picked out, a scarce half mile down the parkway from my family home.

As with so many other ludicrous notions, suicide has always felt like a completely logical life option for me. I could hurt beyond what an alcoholic blackout would numb; I could go through the drama of another failed relationship; or I could just kill myself. I first attempted suicide when I was fourteen. I slit my wrists (poorly). There were several other attempts through the years, the famous cries for help of the person who doesn't really want to die. There were answers to those cries but I usually had moved on to the next bad idea before I could or would accept the help the Lord sent my way.

The help that was available just in this first hospital experience could have been everything I needed to live a pretty normal life afterward. I had presented my highly-agitated, tearful self to the emergency room staff, announcing that I had a suicide plan and I was ready to use it.

After a number of questionnaires and tests, interviews and check-in procedures, I met with a psychiatrist.

He said, "Mrs. Prentiss, I believe you are deeply depressed."

I said, "Dr. Manlove, I believe you must be absolutely brilliant to have figured that out. I think I put that down on one of these many forms you've had me fill out."

"But I believe there is more," he patiently responded. "You have periods of euphoria and elevated moods that indicate more. We believe you are manic depressive."

I sensed what felt like tumblers falling into place: Manic depressive. The monster had a name. Everything I thought I knew would forever be filtered through another lens.

First, I'm a Bible believing Christian in a secular humanist world. That makes me odd.

Now I'm mentally ill. Great. That makes me crazy odd.

I participated in an inpatient program for two months and then went to work, medicated to the gills and all bright and shiny new. And brittle, vulnerable and frayed; I was back in another two months.

Armed with psychiatric jargon and experience I could usually get a general practitioner to prescribe whatever medication I suggested to make me feel okay. I still had my own drugs and alcohol so I could self-medicate, which I did for years. I wasn't ready to have a healing relationship with a psychiatrist and psychologist for decades. In the meantime, I just rocked and rolled and wrote.

The best thing I could have done was to truly turn over the brokenness to Jesus. How amazing is His grace that it would have been available to me any time.

There are complicated explanations for "bipolar disease," a neurological syndrome. The National Association for Mental Illness (NAMI) defines bipolar disorders, or manic depression, as "a serious brain disorder that causes shifts in moods, energy and functioning." The NAMI definition further describes an illness manifested by depressed and manic episodes, as well as a mixed state, called hypomania. According to NAMI, in the mixed state mania and depression are simultaneous.

I use quotes because I hate the designation "bipolar." It sounds round and fluffy like a polar bear, playful and friendly. It is none of the above. I like to call it manic depression because my experience has been like battling a lurid, slimy maniac. However, I use "bipolar" almost exclusively now because it has passed thoroughly into common usage.

It's a matter of mood gone mad. It feels very much like a rollercoaster ride with exhilarating highs and bottomless lows. In between, the cars may roll along smoothly or wobble precariously in a mixed state of high and low. The mixed state feels like driving a very fast car directly toward a brick wall while engaged in full-body, gut-wrenching sobs interspersed with vile invectives.

That's how I felt for about three months before my career blew up. The editor said I was the most negative person he'd ever known, and he didn't know the half of it.

The other half occurred when I went home to my loving husband and teen-aged daughter. In that mixed state I was just raw and ready to attack. My verbal assault weapon was cocked and ready to go. (I'm not physically violent, except toward myself; I think I understand the impulses of those who are.) "Lashing out" implies that the lasher whips the victim, but in my condition in the fall of 2003, my insults were designed to *decapitate* the victim.

My daughter was only fourteen years old. My husband and I had been married seven years. Because I had never honestly faced the monster before October 2003, we all had to do so at the same time.

I was losing all sense of myself in the mood swings, the loss of judgment and the inability to function. I think other bipolar persons feel this way, but I'm lucky to keep friends at all, no less bipolar friends, so I don't really know. There are books about bipolars, but they are usually about celebrities, so I don't feel much kinship or understanding there. But if I can take the license to speak for others, I'd say we never know which end of the ride we're on and whether we're facing to the front or to the rear in our cars. Even when we're feeling pretty good we don't necessarily feel comfortable in our skins. What is normal for me? Is another depression coming? Or am I going to begin another manic phase where I beat up those who are closest to me? Or hurt myself? One thing's for sure, without conscientious lifetime treatment, rolling along smoothly is not an option for very long.

Every state in which we find ourselves seems totally rational to us.

Depression, when we are unable to stop crying, when we cannot face the sun, cannot answer the phone, cannot leave the bed, seems rational. We may eat junk food in bed and watch old movies or neglect to eat at all. Seems rational.

And every manic episode contains the seeds of a horrible, mind-numbing consequence within it. When you are in the middle of it, that high state seems completely rational to you. But it is not rational, it's chemical, and it doesn't come for free.

I cried every night and every day from Dec. 15, 2003 to February 24, 2004, and I thought it was perfectly rational. Nobody died, I wasn't in physical pain, I just cried from a place deep inside. Every day for sixty-eight days.

Although it is irrational for us to believe that we don't really need to eat or sleep, we have believed it, and had many other delusions as well. Like what? Well, in the moments when one's mind races the fastest, it seems perfectly sane to buy a late model BMW, even if you've just gotten your first promotion from flipping burgers to running the cash register. It seems rational.

It must be said, there are reasons to have mood swings other than having bipolar disorder, because every life has ups and downs.

Imagine a woman sitting at her desk at the bank and she gets the news—a distant uncle has left his considerable estate to her, no strings attached. Instant euphoria!

Picture a freshman college student who opens his first semester report card to learn he's going to have to work harder than he did in high school to get those good grades. Instant depression!

There are at least two differences between these examples and the experience of person with bipolar disorder. Basically, these are two people who usually walk on the sidewalk but take a brief ride on the rollercoaster.

First of all, for the sidewalk person, there was reason for the change in mood. That bank employee had every reason to feel the giddiness of sudden, extreme wealth. The freshman who was first in his high school graduating class got a little kick in the pants. It bruises a tender ego.

Secondly, if they are healthy, the bank employee and the student quickly bounce back. That euphoria will level out once the bank employee gets the first call from the Internal Revenue Service; the student will come out of his doldrums when he buckles down and carves out a few more hours for study time.

In contrast, for a bipolar the mood swing is a chemical shift. It isn't a circumstance and we do not cause it. And unfortunately, it is not unusual for a bipolar disordered person to take six to eighteen months from the time of diagnosis to gain reasonable amount of recovery, according to NAMI.

God's healing has come to me through the way recommended by the psychiatric community: I am on an impressive set of medications and I practice personal discipline by getting enough sleep, good food and exercise. A psychiatrist prescribes the medication and a licensed clinical social worker helps me figure out how I might operate in a world where only some of us are on a rollercoaster. The medication gives me a fighting chance against the chemical imbalances that will occur no matter how I try to think or act my way out of them. Frequent mood swings are just going to exist as part of my make-up. The talk therapy provides concrete strategies I can employ in order to function in life whether I'm feeling over-bold or overwhelmed.

My emotional reactions to situations are strong and can be debilitating for hours, days or even weeks. Stress affects everyone differently. Especially as I get older, it doesn't take much to shut me down emotionally or to turn me cold and uncaring. Conversely, it doesn't take a tragedy for me to feel the undertow of depression slinking around my ankles, threatening to pull me down. I've learned to live simply in order to preserve energy for what really matters: living in my own skin without harming myself or others, serving faithfully, honoring God. (To act justly and to love mercy and to walk humbly with your God. Micah 6:8 NIV)

Only the blood-scarred hands of Jesus the Christ can truly heal me. He's been faithful to me when I have been wicked, wayward and stubborn. He has worked with me, carrying me, calling me and coming to my aid in the form of many a human angel, a Christian writer, a Bible study or a minister.

I am part of a small church community in a small town. We're Methodist, because the food is excellent and the doctrine is sound. I've been somewhat forthright about my mental illness within my church. While mental illness is not as stigmatized as it once was, let's say it is still pretty mysterious to the uninitiated. So I try to enlighten those I can.

The view from the rollercoaster has often been breathtaking and sometimes I've seen only death at the end of the ride. Glory to Almighty God, now I know when my car finally comes off the track, there will be a third paradigm shift and I'll be going home.

YOU'RE SAVING MY LIFE

In the key of pain

Alexandria, Virginia

I felt smaller than a minute falling through some cosmic floor
To a land of no tomorrow where love could live no more.
So many voices calling me, so many outstretched hands
What the well-meaning could not comprehend
You understood first hand
When my life hung in the balance
You helped me hang in tight
When my heart was all in darkness somehow you flicked the light...

Don't think I don't know, you're saving my life
Don't think I don't appreciate, you're saving my life.
When you took my hand and said, "We'll turn this thing around"
For the first time in my life I knew my feet could find the ground

Do you know that I know Please know that I know
You've gotta gotta know, You're Saving My Life.

At twenty-six, with a broken heart, some women
might have written this to a new lover. I was a woman
who had developed a knowledge of the saving grace of
Jesus Christ and I'd like to say I wrote the song for Him.
But that would be a lie. I could not yet appreciate that
Jesus was offering to provide the healing through the
hands of doctors.

Really, friends, I wrote the song for the first shrink
who named the demon, Dr. Manlove.

I am grateful that I didn't take in my guitar and try
to assault the poor guy with my brand-new songwriting
skills. You should be grateful this book doesn't come
with a CD.

BREAST CANCER

Liberty, Indiana—Most people, by the time they've reached their 40's, probably have some chronic disease or another to cope with, and it is a fortunate life that hasn't been touched by tragedy.

On August 11, 2004, six months after my last hospital admission for a bipolar episode, I was diagnosed with an aggressive lobular breast cancer. Since it's nothing but the top of the line for me, it had advanced to Stage 4 very quickly. Very quickly, we made decisions. I had a bilateral mastectomy and chemotherapy.

Chemotherapy required no change in my psychiatric medication schedule, thank God. I don't know what would have happened if I'd had to face manic or depressive episodes during the cancer therapy. I'm grateful, too, that I had the example of my mother and my sister, who had both had mastectomies and survived their battles with breast cancer. I was able to tell my daughter, and myself, that we just don't die from breast cancer in our family.

On August 11, 2009, my husband Frank and daughter Claire decked out our dining room in pink roses and red zinnias and we celebrated the fifth anniversary of my—our—survival.

Between the cancer and the anniversary, my parents had a fatal car accident; Daddy died one week after the crash and Mom lived on for eleven painful months.

They built their vacation dream house decades earlier and it was there they were heading when the accident occurred.

Back when they first built the house, I had been diagnosed with bipolar and was dabbling around with treatment. I still enjoyed the manic highs way too much to consider medication and I certainly wasn't going to talk about it with a psychologist! "The Dune" was first published in a Richmond, Virginia literary magazine while I was in college in my late twenties. (Uh, that would be the fifth time I was enrolled in college...) The beach house was a refuge from my internal misery and a place to feel closer to God.

After writing "The Dune" I never again considered the house or the Dune as a permanent point of reference. I had seen its vulnerability. My reference point is Christ the Rock and my view will more than likely always be from this bipolar rollercoaster. Bipolar illness is a chronic disease and so, for that matter, is breast cancer. Chronic as in "it doesn't go away and it might get worse." But it doesn't define me.

In reviewing "The Dune" for this book, I recognized what I had known since that first paradigm shift in the parking lot. God is true, absolute and ageless. We can attempt to fortify ourselves from our pain and hide behind our self-invented truths or we can choose to believe the way, the truth and the life. That truth saved my life. And the ocean that I once viewed with fear I now see as God's first creation, where the Spirit moved and still moves with healing winds of grace.

THE DUNE

Duck, North Carolina—It is nearly sunset as I drive my 1979 Chevrolet Malibu station wagon, also known as my "Chariot of Embers," on to the concrete slab. The plan is to get a cup of coffee in my hands and watch the sun drop into the Currituck Sound. It is all the agenda I have for at least forty-eight hours and I think it's a good one. I turn off the ignition. It only takes a few minutes for the engine to stop sputtering.

No need for me to look around my vacation cottage. I've been coming to the house at Duck, North Carolina, for six years now, ever since my parents built it, which they did despite my howls of derision and mutters of skepticism.

"Read the Bible, Daddy. 'Don't build you house on the sand.' Yes, I know it's a parable. Parable sort of rhymes with rubble, yeah? This isn't real estate, folks, this is a sand dune."

My parents are extremely forgiving folk, not given to retribution in kind, so I have my own keys to the 4-bed-room, 2 ½ bath, wall-to-wall carpeted, juniper paneled, cathedral-ceilinged, track-lit house they named the "Outer Banks Statement." In beach real estate, they call this a cottage.

Even my folks visit the cottage only in the off season. During the summer, I camp out far to the south, as behooves my poverty. The in-season rental income probably has a great deal to do with my parents' contention that it's no problem to finance my senior year of college fully 16 years after they financed my freshman year. So I've mellowed, learned to show a little respect for their real estate acumen and excellent taste. I have also come to love the cottage. It is probably the grandest place I'll ever lay my head.

I've long since stopped looking at the underside of the structure. In my howling days, the engineers in the family convinced me that I didn't know enough about their craft to observe what they knew. And what they knew was that this cottage is "massively overbuilt."

It seems that Ken Green, the builder, was a new kid on the block when he contracted to construct our cottage. His reputation was on the line, and he left no weather- or erosion-proofing to chance. The current state of the art in beach construction leans heavily on the disasters of the past. So the timbers that act as stilts are driven 20 feet down into the sand. Somehow Green gave the house some ability to sway with the wind instead of standing entirely against it, the bend instead of break principle that works so well for trees. Although the building code calls for only every third rafter to be steel strapped and bolted to the frame, Green treated every rafter this way. No roof from one of his cottages is going to sail off during a hurricane or nor'easter. Around the outside perimeter of the stilts at the 8.5 foot level, not only the required two, but three levels of 2" X 12" salt-treated wood are bolted to the pilings, providing more stability, adding to the "massive overbuilding."

As I said, we'd been through this years ago, and the conversations are recorded in my journal in only slightly skeptical tones. "Massively overbuilt." That's the comforting phrase that has seduced me through the years.

Now I just let myself in, brew a pot of decaf, head for the porch and absorb the brilliance of the sound-side sunset. When the show is over, I go about the business of unloading lots of musical instruments (no textbooks) and two sleepy cats from the wagon. I unpack a week's worth of jeans and sweatshirts into the dresser in the upstairs bedroom I like the best, the one closest to the fireplace. I like the view of the ocean from my bed.

The master suites downstairs don't allow that view because of The Dune.

The Dune is very special to oceanfront landowners. The barrier islands of Virginia and the Carolinas are extremely fragile. Those islands, known as the Outer Banks, are only five or six miles wide at their widest. Duck, North Carolina, where the cottage affords a view of both the sea and the Currituck Sound, is not one of the widest points. It is The Dune, we believe, that makes our property so much safer than property down in, say, Kitty Hawk or Kill Devil Hills, several miles to the south.

It's dark when I finish the housekeeping tasks. I retune my guitar and autoharp and build a fire.

Peering through the salted windows on the ocean side it is hard to distinguish The Dune from the sea. I turn on the flood lights, illuminating only the porch. Not worth the electricity, I think, and turn them off again. I can see a little of The Dune, the part immediately in front of the cottage anyway, even without the lights. Its covering of sea grass is thick and brown and cowlicked from the recent high winds. The sea grass holds The Dune in place, you see, and later in the week I will explain to young houseguests that we never, never, never walk on The Dune because it so very fragile and because it is all that is between our cottage and the mean old ocean. We walk instead on an access ramp that spans The Dune and provides a 15-step staircase down to the beach.

It's later, after I've played around with a very old Bob Dylan tune for a few hours, that I bank the fire and go to bed, safe in the massively overbuilt timbers, secure behind The Dune. The songs I sing before I sleep sing back to me until I do. Tonight the accompaniment is the sea.

The ocean in the morning is a very fine thing, as I look out from the window, there behind The Dune.

Wait a minute. The access ramp, as designed, leads across our property, up The Dune, and crests it. Now, not by design, it hangs there, the bench at the top bobbing slightly in the stiff breeze.

I run down the stairs to the first floor porch, whip around the corner, down the stairs to the slab, across the yard, up to the ramp to the top of The Dune.

It is not at all the gentle hummock I thought I saw the night before, but instead drops from its crest down a 15-foot cliff straight to the beach. The sea grass (it holds The Dune down, you know) is wrapped in tight little balls embedded in this shifting cliff. The bench— I have photos of myself waving to the cottage from that bench—sticks out from the cliff like a tongue depressor. I look up and down the beach from my clifftop. Not a single beach ramp exists as far as I can see to the south. Toward the north I think I see one intact.

I walk up the street behind the houses until I reach the ramp that looked whole. It isn't. The drop here is only five feet or so, but even more ominous. Because here, instead of mere sea grass, there is thick, gnarly maritime forest undergrowth to hold The Dune. It, too, is embedded in the cliff face as casually as the puny sea grass in front of our cottage.

I walk back through the streets to the cottage. I enter from the carport, the concrete slab, the massively over-built underbelly of the cottage built on the sand.

I haven't even taken a walk on the beach yet, but the ocean seems very, very close as I eat my breakfast.

I pull out after breakfast to find a couple weeks worth of local news coverage. That would be the Coastal Times and the North Carolina section of the Virginian

Pilot, but since there is no library in Dare County I have to drive to Roanoke Island to read the news.

I learn a great deal about what happened to the ramp and to The Dune. Three storms from the northeast in two weeks time. Hurricanes cause wind damage but nor'easters cause erosion and the damage tolls rose with each day's report. The final report was that 313 cottages were destroyed, damaged or condemned.

The local politicians really made hay while the sun shown and the winds died between storms, demanding that Gov. Jim Martin declare disaster and come see firsthand the extreme erosion under the Herbert C. Bonner Bridge. The bridge spans Oregon Inlet to Hatteras Island, and the preservation of said bridge is a hot political potato. Two hundred feet of erosion in three weeks was alleged to have made quite an impression on the Governor's deputy.

Winds of 58 miles per hour and 15- to 20-foot seas were reported on March 9. It was also noted that it was 27 years to the day of the Ash Wednesday storm, the benchmark storm by which all Atlantic Coast residents measured every other storm.

It was further noted that the police had protected the beaches from looters for nearly a week and today, March 13, is the first day there is unrestricted access to NC12, known to native and tourist alike as the Beach Road.

The day is cold and raw, but the Chariot is warm as I drive back toward Duck on the Beach Road. The sea looks like a summer's day, blue and breaking gently in long clean waves. Surfers would call it a great day. Surely, I thought, there would be no surfers in this wet wind.

From the road the damage doesn't look so bad—occasionally a roadside cottage is surrounded by yellow plastic tape printed with big black letters that read: FIRE LINE DO NOT CROSS. But the structures seem to be upright at any rate.

The Clay Don Motor Lodge in Kitty Hawk, mentioned in several of the news articles, is the first shocker. It consisted of three duplexes and a central office in a separate building, all trimmed in aqua and yellow siding over a stucco-type wall. It is, or was, a modest accommodation for a family who cares more about the beach than wall-to-wall carpeting. As with about half the structures here in the southern end, the Clay Don is not on stilts. The two buildings next to the road, swathed in yellow plastic tape, look fine, but even from the road I can see the third building split right in two as the sea ate the sand out from under it. A bed and jagged dresser are visible through the torn wall. The angle of the sea side half of the broken duplex is familiar—it looks like our ramp.

Beyond the Clay Don, wet-suited surfers are barreling through frothy breakers after all.

As I get out I notice the cottage next to the Clay Don for the first time. It looks reasonably upright.

There is a pink paper sign stapled to its wall, though, no more than six inches square, which outlines in dignified legalese several variations on the theme, stated boldly across the bottom, that "THIS BUILDING NOT SAFE FOR HABITATION." Condemned.

"The septic tank, it broke right in two," says the man working on the cottage. His face is so grizzled, his hands so raw, his irritation at fate, the surfers and me is so obvious that I don't have the nerve to ask his name. All I can muster is one question.

"How long has the Clay Don been here?" Stupid question at that.

"Since the 1940's. Been just fine since the 40's." He glares. I trudge back to the road, back to my warm car.

I had been close enough to observe that his cottage was not massively overbuilt.

If I had an audience, I am ashamed to say, I would be wisecracking about the unfortunate names of the cottages, which, as I drive north through Kitty Hawk, are increasingly festooned with yellow plastic tape and little pink condemnation notices.

"Sea Retreat." (Not really.). "By the Sea." (Almost in the sea, actually). Sure. Pretty funny. Except that as I drive north, the more I see evidence that these cottages, if not massively overbuilt, are carefully constructed.

Parking at the Kitty Hawk Bath House is a fairly dicey decision. The Chariot barely has tread on the tires, much less traction to escape the sand that piles across the lot. But I have to see this stretch of beach, partly because I have a baseline pictures of how it looked in summer. And I want to send pictures to a friend who has a condo nearby and who would probably appreciate an eyewitness report.

One of the quotes from the Coastal Times comes back to me: "There was enough lumber washed ashore at Oregon Inlet to build 40 cottages." Here on this 100-yard stretch before me there is enough lumber to build at least one. Not driftwood, but huge timbers, the type that get pounded 20 feet into the sand and serve as stilts. Massive. And today, with the various localities issuing scavenger permits for the first time since the storm, there are trucks on the beach. A sworn enemy of 4-wheel drive vehicles on the beach, I understand for the first time their utility. You need them to pick up the pieces.

From the beach, the ocean's powerful clawing pull and the wind's twisted scathing currents left their mark on the backs of structures that, when I saw them from the front, had looked merely messy. On their beach sides, they are forever altered.

A porch that had once spanned the entire length of the house had corkscrewed up to the middle, taking up only a third of its original length. Behind the porch, a miraculously intact plate glass window reveals a lamp hanging across the window on a diagonal. The whole structure is leaning 50 degrees away from the beach.

Open drain pipes stick out of those new sand cliffs. Some stairs lead from a house and end at a point six feet above the dirty sand. Another set of steps rises from the sand intact only to arrive at nothing.

On the beach itself, an oven had been pile-driven upside down, 20 inches into the sand. It was rusted, and had no doors or hinges.

It was, if I have ever seen one, a massively overbuilt oven.

The Chariot rises to the occasion and pulls smartly out of the public parking lot. The drive from Kitty Hawk to Duck seems shorter than it ever has. I don't want the destruction of the Clay Don to be as close to our property as it is. In fact it is nine short miles.

The southern part of the Outer Banks, from South Nags Head to Southern Shores, has been developed, as the disgruntled homeowner had reminded me, for several decades before the building boom that developed Duck and points north.

Karen Ellege, of Real Escapes Real Estate in Duck, points out that what had been learned from the southern developments had been applied to the northern ones. Each township, progressing north, made its setback requirements longer, compelling each builder to move farther back from the ocean. And, she twinkled, we have The Dune.

Twenty-four hours after my arrival at Duck, I once again bump the aging Chevy onto the slab beneath the bedroom where I would sleep. I look at those timbers, braces, beams and bolts. I notice a bracket had rusted out, leaving a water pipe unsupported and sagging. I find half a shingle on the slab. Green, like our roof. (Since there had been a protracted community debate over the scandalous green roof my parents—those rebels—had desired, and since they prevailed in that debate, I know the shingle is indeed from our own massively overbuilt cottage.)

I go upstairs. The cats wake up. I build a fire and the cats doze again. I brew tea, start some soup. I watch another brilliant sunset over the Currituck Sound. I keep my back to the ocean and my eyes on the splendid fiesta sky. I pick up my harp as the sky goes charcoal gray.

Here's the thing: Larger forces shape our lives. Perhaps the seas of the world are rising, perhaps not; but the islands shift and inlets come and go. Where I lay my head tonight may not be there tomorrow.

Our massively overbuilt lives are not guaranteed. The lady whose life savings provide the bed I sleep in tonight says this: "It is not a matter of if the sea comes in. It's a matter of when the sea comes in."

Thanks, Mom.

The ocean sounds very close to my ears tonight. This is not poetic license, but an observation as true as the upside-down oven, the twisted porch, the tongue-depressor access ramp. The ocean is very close tonight.

www.ingramcontent.com/pod-product-compliance
Lightning Source LLC
Chambersburg PA
CBHW060633280326
41933CB00012B/2019